Second Edition

Learning World 2
WORKBOOK

four 4 4

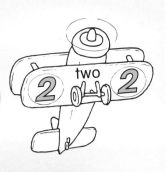

two 2 2

5 five 5

one 1 1

10 ten 10

6 six 6

JN122194

pink
red
orange
yellow
green
blue
purple
brown
black
gray
white

9 nine 9

three 3 3

8 eight 8

7 seven 7

upper case

lower case

upper case

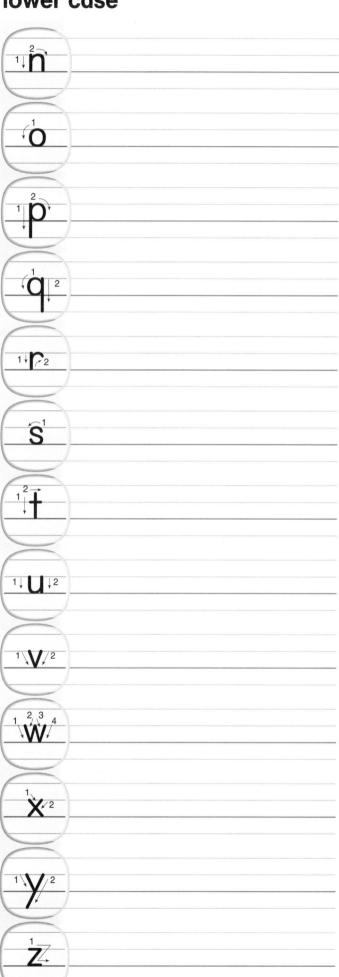

N

O

P

Q

R

S

T

U

V

W

X

Y

Z

lower case

n

o

p

q

r

s

t

u

v

w

x

y

z

書きじゅんに決まりはありません。
この書きじゅんは1つのれいです。

1 Write the upper case letter.

lower case   upper case

1 book ⟷

2 house ⟷

3 apple ⟷

4 pencil ⟷

5 eraser ⟷

2 Can you write about yourself?

Hello!   My name is   .

I'm   years old.   I live in   .

Write the sentences on your own.

1	**2**	**3**	**4**	**5**	**6**	**7**	**8**	**9**	**10**	**11**	**12**
one	two	three	four	five	six	seven	eight	nine	ten	eleven	twelve

⬤ Color the flags and choose the alphabet in the map.

1
red ········
red ········
······· white
Canada ( )

2
blue ········
······· white
······· red
France ( )

3
yellow ········
······· red
China ( )

4
black ········
white ········
green ········
······· red
······· white
Kenya ( )

5
······· black
······· red
······· yellow
Germany ( )

6
······· red
······· yellow
······· red
Spain ( )

7
red ········
······· black
······· blue
······· white
Korea ( )

8
white ········
······· red
······· blue
······· red
Thailand ( )

9
······· orange
······· white
······· green
India ( )

10
light blue ········
······· yellow
······· green
Brazil ( )

11
······· red
······· white
Japan ( )

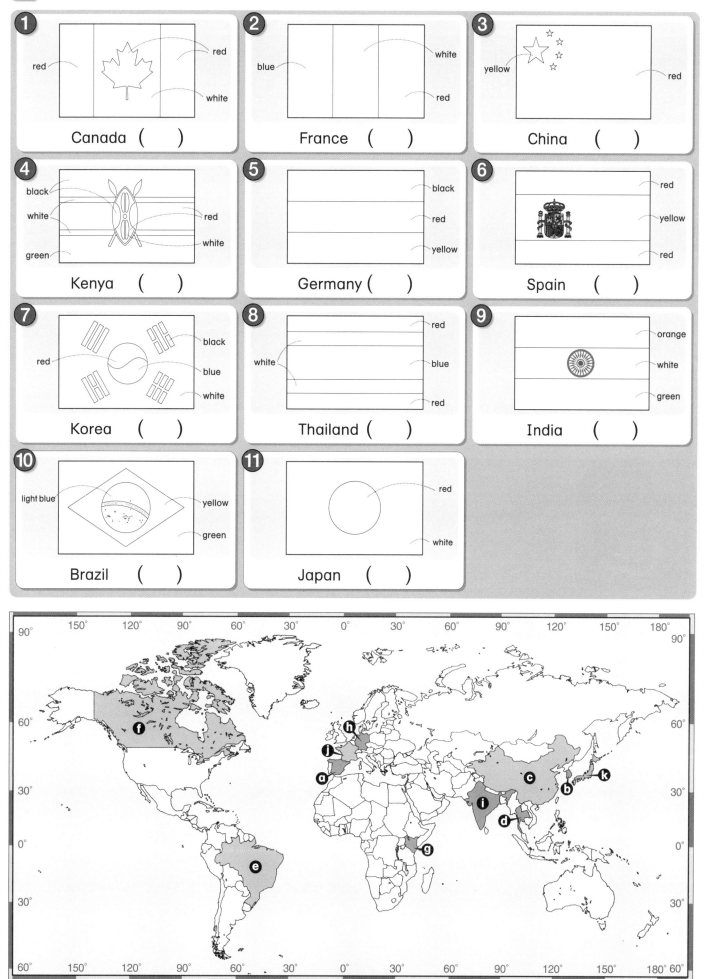

He (His)   **She (Her)**

1

What's his name?

His name is _____

Where is he from?

He is from _____

2

What's her name?

Her name _____

Where is she from?

She is _____

3

What's her name?

_____

Where is she from?

_____

4

What's her name?

_____

Where is she from?

_____

5

What's his name?

_____

Where is he from?

_____

Write the first letter.

1  _____ pple

7  _____ host

2  _____ ook

8  _____ ouse

3  _____ at

9  _____ nk

4  _____ og

10  _____ ack-o'-lantern

5  _____ lephant

11  _____ ing

6 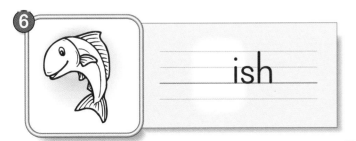 _____ ish

12  _____ ion

1 Find and color.

1 A red cat is **sleeping**.

2 A blue cat is **dancing**.

3 A green cat is **singing**.

4 A yellow cat is **swimming**.

5 A pink cat is **running**.

6 A brown cat is **flying**.

7 A black cat is **reading**.

8 A purple cat is **eating**.

running   swimming   flying   reading   sleeping   eating   singing   dancing

2 What are we doing?

Draw your face.   I   We   Draw your face.   You   He   She

1 What is he doing?

He is

2 What is she doing?

She is

3 What are you doing?

We are

2

1 **Connect the pictures to the sentences.**

Yumi is fine.

Mark is sleepy.

Ema is angry.

Min is tired.

We are happy.

Nelson is hungry.

2 **Yes, (s)he is. ／ No, (s)he isn't.**

① Is Mark angry?

② Is Min tired?

③ Is Yumi hungry?

④ Is Nelson happy?

⑤ Is Ema angry?

1 Color the stars.

① Color four little stars yellow.

② Color three big stars yellow.

③ Color two big stars green.

④ Color one big star red.

⑤ Color five little stars green.

⑥ Color seven little stars red.

2 See the textbook p.14 and fill in the blanks.

① Min's kite — It is a little red triangle.

② Ema's kite — It is a

③ Nelson's kite —

④ Mark's kite —

⑤ Yumi's kite —

4

◎ Choose the correct answer.

1 あさ、あいさつする時 (Greeting in the morning)
- ① Good evening.
- ② Good morning.
- ③ Good night.
- ④ Thank you.

2 ありがとうと言われた時 (When someone says thank you)
- ① Thank you.
- ② Yes, I do.
- ③ You're welcome.
- ④ I'm hungry.

3 ほしくないものをすすめられた時 (Declining someone's offer)
- ① No, I don't.
- ② No, you are not.
- ③ No, I am not.
- ④ No, thank you.

4 曜日を聞く時 (Asking the day of the week)
- ① What time is it?
- ② What is the date today?
- ③ What day is it today?
- ④ What is your name?

5 ねる時のあいさつ (What you say before you go to sleep)
- ① Good-bye.
- ② Good morning.
- ③ Good night.
- ④ Good bed.

6 初めて人に会った時 (Meeting someone for the first time)
- ① Nice to meet you.
- ② Good night.
- ③ I'm fine, thank you.
- ④ See you later.

7 わすれものをした時 (When you forgot something)
- ① Thank you.
- ② I forgot.
- ③ I'm finished.
- ④ No, thank you.

1

What time do you wake up?

I wake up at

2

What time do you go to school?

I go to school at

3

What time do you go home?

4

What time do you do your homework?

5

What time do you take a bath?

6

What time do you go to bed?

I have twelve dollars. I want a ....

I want a _____ with _____

I want a _____ with _____

I want a _____ with _____

I want a _____ with _____

I want a _____ with _____

I want a _____ with _____

 2 dollars single

 4 dollars double

 **6** dollars triple

⊙ What is there?

1

a cat	a dog	a bat
a pen	a pin	a hat
a mop	a can	a hen
a cap	a cup	a ten
a man	a map	a six

2

a cat	a dog	a bat
a pen	a pin	a hat
a mop	a can	a hen
a cap	a cup	a ten
a man	a map	a six

ANIMAL BINGO

1 Say the words and color.

① lion
② hippo
③ bear
④ dog
⑤ rabbit
⑥ duck
⑦ snake
⑧ cow
⑨ dinosaur
⑩ fox
⑪ tiger
⑫ cat
⑬ elephant
⑭ monkey
⑮ spider

2 Write the words and make your own Bingo Board.

1 Look at the timetable and answer.

have / don't have

Monday	Tuesday	Wednesday	Thursday	Friday
English	music	Japanese	social studies	math
math	Japanese	math	Japanese	Japanese
science	science	social studies	math	P.E.
P.E.	arts & crafts	music	music	
	arts & crafts		science	
	social studies			

① I have / don't have math on Tuesday.

② I have / don't have English on Friday.

③ I _____ science on Wednesday.

④ I _____ Japanese on Monday.

2 Complete the sentences about yourself.

like / don't like

① I _____ math.

② I _____ Japanese.

③ I _____ music.

1 Choose the correct answer.

1 Do you have a dog?   Yes, I am.   Yes, I do.   Yes, it is.

2 Do you want a dog?   Yes, I am.   Yes, I do.   Yes, it is.

3 Do you like dogs?   Yes, I am.   Yes, I do.   Yes, it is.

4 What is your brother's name?

I am Takashi.
My name is Takashi.
His name is Takashi.

2 Complete the sentences about yourself.

1 I (have, don't have) a dog.

I (want, don't want) a dog.

I (like, don't like) dogs.

2 I (have, don't have) a cat.

I (want, don't want) a cat.

I (like, don't like) cats.

3 I (have, don't have) a dinosaur.

I (want, don't want) a dinosaur.

I (like, don't like) dinosaurs.

4 I (have, don't have) a bat.

I (want, don't want) a bat.

I (like, don't like) bats.

Fill in the missing letter.

1. p _ n
2. m _ p
3. n _ t
4. h _ p
5. h _ t
6. f _ n
7. b _ t
8. b _ d
9. c _ p

10. l _ p
11. s _ t
12. f _ x
13. s _ n
14. r _ n
15. m _ n
16. c _ p
17. m _ p
18. h _ n

I have a pet snake. It is green and red. It is not scary.
It is long. It is in a black box. I like it very much.

1 Fill in the blanks.

1 I have _____

2 It is _____

3 It is _____

4 It is _____

5 It is in _____

6 I _____ it very much.

2 Answer the questions.

1 What do you have? _____

2 What color is it? _____

3 Is it scary? _____

4 Is it short? _____

5 Where is it? _____

6 Do you like it? _____

1 Look at the pictures and write the answers.

1

Where are you?

I'm in the

2

Where are you?

3

Where are you?

4

Where are you?

5

Where are you?

2 Based on p.28 of the textbook, complete the dialogue.

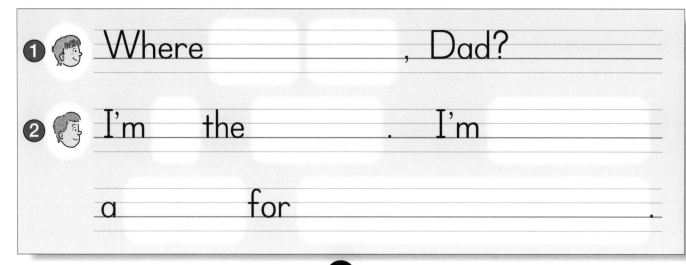

① Where _____, Dad?

② I'm ___ the _____. I'm _____

a _____ for _____.

1 **Write the answers.**

Yes, I do. / No, I don't.

1 Do you like cucumbers? _____

2 Do you like onions? _____

3 Do you like carrots? _____

4 Do you like broccoli? _____

5 Do you like spinach? _____

2 **Complete the sentences about yourself.**

1 I (don't like, like) spinach.

2 I (don't like, like) lettuce.

3 I (don't like, like) broccoli.

4 I (don't like, like) cabbage.

5 I (don't like, like) onions.

6 I (don't like, like) corn.

7 I (don't like, like) carrots.

8 I (don't like, like) green peppers.

1 Fill in the blanks.

I want

_____ , _____ ,

_____ , _____ and

_____ for my supper.

2 Choose and write words to make 18 points.

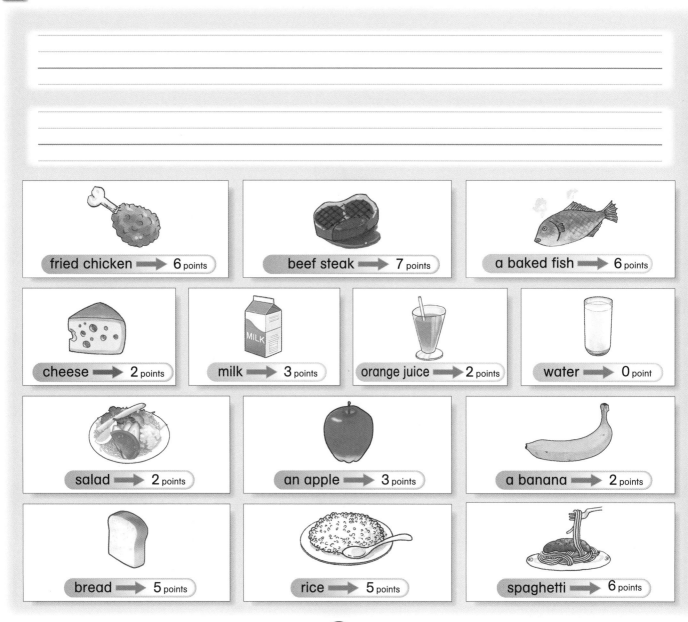

fried chicken ➡ 6 points

beef steak ➡ 7 points

a baked fish ➡ 6 points

cheese ➡ 2 points

milk ➡ 3 points

orange juice ➡ 2 points

water ➡ 0 point

salad ➡ 2 points

an apple ➡ 3 points

a banana ➡ 2 points

bread ➡ 5 points

rice ➡ 5 points

spaghetti ➡ 6 points

1 **Say the words and color.**

1. blouse
2. cap
3. hat
4. pajamas
5. skirt
6. shorts
7. sweater
8. socks
9. sneakers
10. shoes
11. pants
12. raincoat
13. shirt
14. belt
15. dress

2 **Write the words and make your own Bingo Board.**

Connect the dots and write the sentences.

1 Comb your hair.

2 Put on your shoes.

3 Brush your teeth.

4 Dry your face.

5 Wash your face.

6 Pack your bag.

I comb my hair.

1 Circle each phrase using the colors below.

Where → red When → blue How → yellow

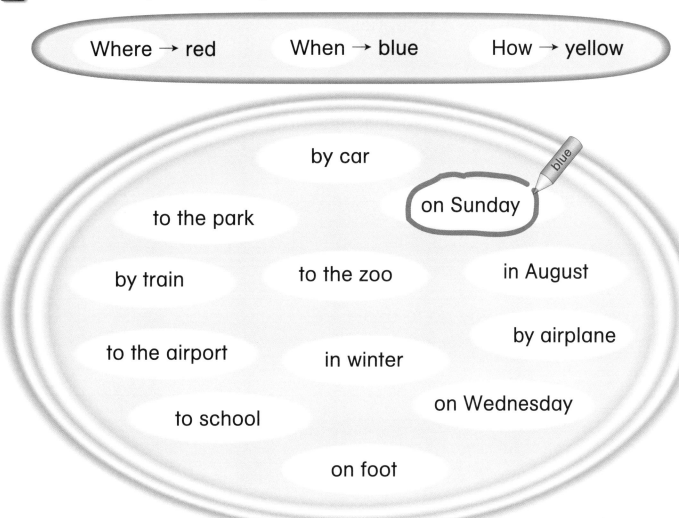

by car

on Sunday

to the park

by train   to the zoo   in August

to the airport   in winter   by airplane

on Wednesday

to school

on foot

2 Let's make sentences using the phrases above.

1 I go

red   yellow   blue

2

3

4

1 **Write the sentences about yourself.**

What time do you eat supper?

1 I eat supper at

What time do you do your homework?

2 I do my homework

What time do you take a bath?

3

What time do you go to bed?

4

2

before
(⟶)

after
(⟵)

1 I brush my teeth _____ I eat breakfast.
(   )

2 I change my clothes _____ I eat breakfast.
(   )

3 I take a bath _____ I do my homework.
(   )

4 I do my homework _____ I eat supper.
(   )

5 I wash my body _____ I wash my hair.
(   )

I am a bird. I am pretty. I have two wings.
I can fly. I like flowers.

1 Fill in the blanks.

1 I am _____

2 I am _____

3 I have _____

4 I can _____

5 I like _____

2 Answer the questions.

1 What are you?
_____

2 How many wings do you have?
_____

3 What can you do?
_____

4 What do you like?
_____

5 Are you pretty?
_____

6 Do you have wings?
_____

7 Can you fly?
_____

Unit 7 ①

1 How is the weather today?

| fine | sunny | cool | cold | hot | windy | snowy | cloudy | rainy |

2 Choose and circle.

1 How is the weather?
- a) It is summer.
- b) It is sunny.
- c) Yes, it is.

2 What time is it?
- a) It is seven o'clock.
- b) It is a clock.
- c) No, it isn't.

3 What is the date?
- a) It is Monday today.
- b) It is June 20th today.
- c) It is sunny today.

4 What day is it today?
- a) It is Monday today.
- b) It is June 20th today.
- c) It is sunny today.

1 Color the bats.

- A sad bat on the bench is red.
- A sad bat on the table is black.
- A happy bat under the bench is pink.
- A happy bat under the table is brown.
- An angry bat on the bench is orange.
- An angry bat under the table is purple.

happy   sad   angry

2 Answer the questions.

1 What color is the happy bat under the bench?

It is

2 What color is the angry bat on the bench?

3 What color is the sad bat on the bench?

4 What color is the happy bat under the table?

5 What color is the sad bat on the table?

6 What color is the angry bat under the table?

What do you have in your bag?

1  I have three textbooks, a notebook and a key in my bag. ( )

2  I have two notebooks, five pencils and an eraser in my bag. ( )

3  I have a game, two comic books and a notebook in my bag. ( )

4  I have two books, three pencils and a key in my bag. ( )

5  I have a handkerchief, two keys and an eraser in my bag. ( )

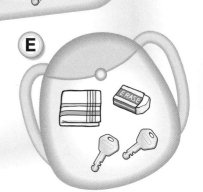

SCHOOL BINGO

1 **Say the words and color.**

① desk	② stapler	③ pencil	④ eraser	⑤ ruler
⑥ bag	⑦ book	⑧ textbook	⑨ clock	⑩ blackboard
⑪ chair	⑫ scissors	⑬ teacher	⑭ pencil case	⑮ chalk

2 **Write the words and make your own Bingo Board.**

1 Will you ...?

1 open the door

Will you _____ ?

2 leave the window open

3 turn on the light

2 Don't....

1 open the window

Don't _____

2 turn off the light

3 close the door

⬤ Complete the sentences.

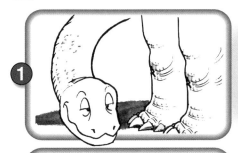

1 What a _____ dinosaur!

2 What a _____ dinosaur!

3 What a _____ dinosaur!

4 _____ !

5 _____ !

6 _____ !

7 _____ !

Yes, you may. × No, you may not.

1. May I sit down?
_____

2. May I use your eraser?
_____

3. May I go out to play?
_____

4. May I eat?
_____

5. May I go to the bathroom?
_____

6. May I open the window?
_____

7. May I turn on the light?
_____

8. May I go to bed?
_____

9. May I turn off the light?
_____

10. May I climb a tree?
_____

I have a monkey. He is black and white.
He can climb a tree. He is wearing a red cap.

1 Fill in the blanks.

1 I have _____

2 He is _____

3 He can _____

4 He is wearing _____

2 Answer the questions.

1 What do you have? _____

2 What color is it? _____

3 What can he do? _____

4 What is he wearing? _____

1 Yumi likes ….

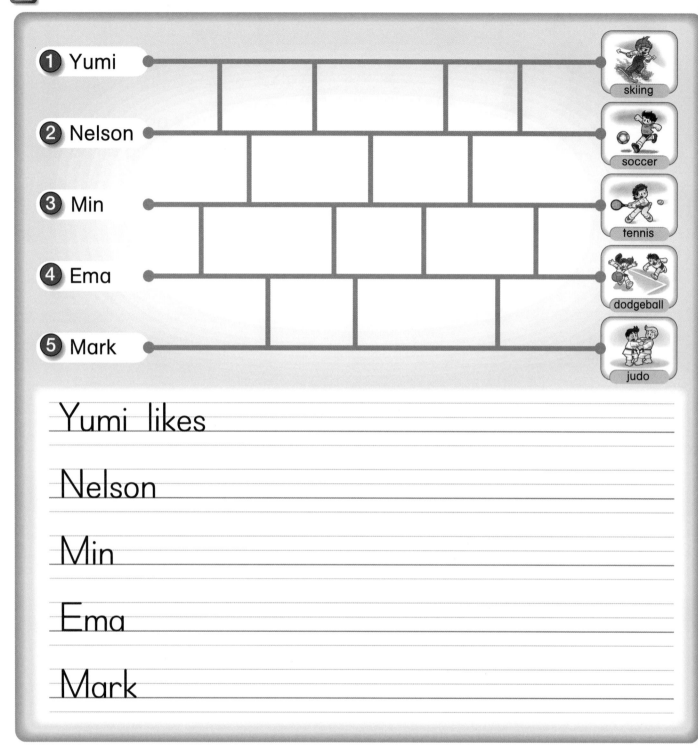

Yumi likes _____

Nelson _____

Min _____

Ema _____

Mark _____

2 What sport do you like? | like / likes |

1 I _____

2 My teacher _____

1 Put the months in order (Japanese seasons).

1 spring months

2 summer months

3 fall months

4 winter months

March   January   April   December   August   February   July   June   October   May   September   November

2 Write the answers on your own.

1 How is the weather today?

2 What time is it now?

3 What is the date?

4 When is your birthday?

1 Write the answers.

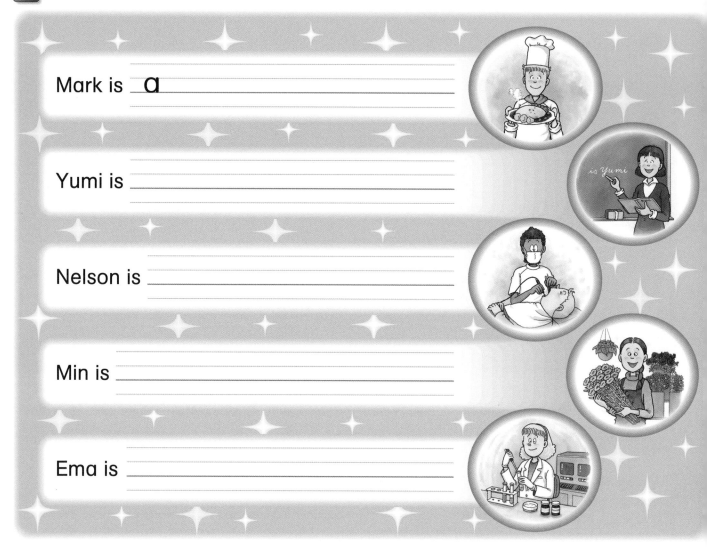

Mark is ___a_____

Yumi is _____

Nelson is _____

Min is _____

Ema is _____

2 Yes, he(she) is. ╱ No, he(she) isn't.

① Is Mark a cook? _____

② Is Yumi a teacher? _____

③ Is Nelson a dentist? _____

④ Is Min a teacher? _____

⑤ Is Ema a florist? _____

I have a big brother. His name is James.

James and I go to the park on Sunday.

We go there by bike. We play tennis in the park.

1 Fill in the blanks.

1 I have _____

2 His name is _____

3 James and I go to _____

4 We go there _____

2 Answer the questions.

1 What is his big brother's name? _____

2 Where do they go? _____

3 When do they go there? _____

4 How do they go there? _____

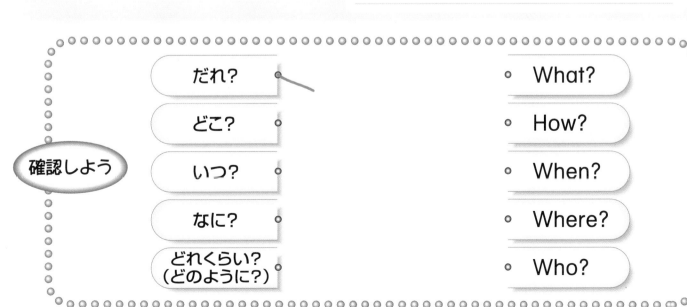

確認しよう

だれ？	What?
どこ？	How?
いつ？	When?
なに？	Where?
どれくらい？ （どのように？）	Who?

Look at the following pictures and answer.

1 2 3 4 5 6

1

① What is the elephant doing?

② Is he hungry?

2

③ What does the elephant find?

3

④ What does the elephant want?

⑤ Can he climb the tree?

4

⑥ Where is the monkey?

5

⑦ What does the monkey say?

6

⑧ What does the elephant say?

Fill in the blanks.

1 In a _____ in the _____ ,

2 A _____ _____ was _____ by _____ _____ .

3 A _____ _____ was _____ by, _____ at the _____ .

4 " _____ _____ , _____ _____ , _____ Before the _____ _____ me dead."

5 The _____ _____ let him in, saying, " _____ _____ , _____ _____ , come inside."

6 " _____ _____ _____ , it is _____ and here _____ _____ hide."

Write your own.

Hello.

1. My name is

2. My family name is

3. I am

4. My birthday is

5. I live in

6. I am from

7. I like

8. I don't like

Complete the sentences and answer the questions.

1 (Where, What) is your name?

2 (Where, What) is your family name?

3 (Where, When) do you live?

4 (How many, How old) are you?

5 (Are, Do) you like apple pie?

6 (How, What) is your mother's name?

7 (Where, What) do you want?

8 (How, Who) do you come to school?

Let's read. ①

Frogs can hop around.
Frogs can swim in water, too.
Baby frogs are tadpoles.
Tadpoles live in water.

● Fill in the blanks.

① Frogs can _____

② Frogs can _____ in water, too.

③ Baby frogs are _____   ④ Tadpoles live _____

● Answer the questions.

① What can frogs do?

_____

② What else can frogs do in water?

_____

③ What are baby frogs?

_____

④ Where do tadpoles live?

_____

⑤ Can frogs hop? _____

⑥ Can frogs fly? _____

⑦ What are tadpoles? _____

Octopuses live in water.
Octopuses are not fish.
Octopuses have eight legs.
Octopuses can swim very well.
Octopuses don't have scales.

● Fill in the blanks.

① Octopuses live _____   ② Octopuses are _____ fish.

③ Octopuses can _____ very well.

④ Octopuses _____ scales.

⑤ Octopuses have _____

● Answer the questions.

① Where do octopuses live?

② What can octopuses do?

③ What do octopuses have?

④ How many legs do octopuses have?

⑤ Are octopuses fish?

⑥ Do octopuses have scales?

Baby butterflies are caterpillars.
Caterpillars eat leaves.
Caterpillars can't fly.
But their fathers and mothers can fly.

● **Fill in the blanks.**

① Baby butterflies are _____

② Caterpillars eat _____

③ Caterpillars _____

④ But their _____ and _____ can fly.

● **Answer the questions.**

① What are baby butterflies?

② What do they eat?

③ Who can fly?

④ Do caterpillars eat leaves?

⑤ Can caterpillars fly?

⑥ What are caterpillars' mothers and fathers?

1 Santa Claus in Canada

Santa is wearing a red cap, a red coat, red pants and red boots.

2 Santa Claus in Australia

Santa is wearing a red T-shirt, red shorts, a red hat and red beach sandals.
He is wearing sunglasses, too.

3 My Santa